Time and Tides

Glimpses of the New Forest in words and pictures

Wendy Stickley

Published 2022
Drop in the Ocean Publications
dropintheocean555@gmail.com

ISBN: 978-1-8383493-1-8

This book is for my family, who have always been my
greatest source of love and support.

Contents

Tides

Two Loves

Ballerina arms of grace
arc and wave, stately, sure;
dressed in lucent vernal lace,
sweep and bow to the forest floor -
beckon ever deeper.

Wave upon wave cavort and chase
each other, rushing up the shore.
Life lived at a different pace,
power and beauty to explore,
beckons ever deeper.

In the forest or by the sea,
near beech or beach, I am truly me.
There breathes wisdom none can see.
Deep calls to deep and sets me free,
beckons ever deeper.

Seasons

New Year

A time to look back on the year that is past
And wonder just how it has vanished so fast;
A time to remember the people I've met,
Hoping that they, too, will not quite forget
Those moments of sunshine and happiness shared
When dreams could be dreamed, and I almost dared
To believe they'd come true. A time to reflect
On the things I've got wrong, resolved to correct
My shortcomings, along with more positive thoughts
Of people and projects that I could support.
This fresh year ahead comes with promise and hope -
A blank, empty slate, with incredible scope
For doing new things and seeing new places,
And meeting the minds behind different new faces.

Winter

No dappled spots where sunshine plays,
No sense of freedom - nothing's right -
Just drab and dreary winter days.

No time to wander country ways
To feel alive and blessed and bright
In dappled spots where sunshine plays.

Darkness descends with misty haze;
People less friendly, less polite
On drab and dreary winter days.

No urge to sing spontaneous praise,
No will to live, no wish to fight,
No dappled spots where sunshine plays.

Muddled, mind-numbed, in this maze,
This endless season of long nights
And drab and dreary winter days.

But wait ... the solstice! Little rays
Of hope, as, day by day, the light
Brings dappled spots where sunshine plays -
And no more drab, drear winter days.

Cry Joy ...

cry joy   for first this dazzling day of spring;
for spray from sparkling water dancing waves;
for dappled growing shadow bluebell-filled
and tadpoled ponds   rainwater ample spilled;
for tiny mighty ants; for colour, plants,
scent, sweetness all-surpassing shocking senses;
for glancing sprightly butterflies around
each other in the bright blue air; for where
green hedgerows   vibrant bursting trees
birds wing   sing   build cosy nests
of fur and feather moss and sticks,
feed hungry chicks all gape and beak
from small soft weak to strong   this springtime
sings the whole wide world along

The Tree

Stark,
with weathered bark.
Bare,
no green or golden leaves
to weave a coat to wear,
or cover angularities.
No true, smooth specimen,
this oak; no tall or upright
citizen. A singularity.

When did it begin? What act
of fate dictated this distorted
shape, this malformed thing?

And yet ... and yet ... for all
the tree's peculiarities,
there is a curious beauty here.
The clear contorted shadows cast
a spell which tethers, binds together,
grass on which it falls, the tree,
and all who pause awhile, who 'stand
and stare'*. They find they can abandon
cares ... perhaps feel whole again.

*from Leisure, by W. H. Davies

On such a day as this

On days like this
when blossom birds full-throated
sing; when bluebells ring their springtime
hymns of sweet woodland; when
earthy shades of vernal green
are seen, life imbibed, new birth
stirring inside; when tadpoles throng
ponds, hedgerows are graced
with Queen Anne's Lace, and cuckoos
harmonise with yaffles yaffling;

on mornings such as these,
sun's rays, a soft and salty breeze,
sea campions and thrift, lift life's groans
from down among the stones
to skylark heights; my soul unites
with all the earth in its rebirth.
On such a day as this there's too
much love inside, it must unfurl
like fern frond curls, it must spread wide,
till it encompasses the world,
flies high (albeit gentle as a sigh)

When I was young

When I was young, summers were hot
And long; snow-filled winters did not
Seem damp and grey; autumn leaves piled ...
And we jumped in; winds made us wild
When I was young.

Doctors seemed old! We ate a lot
Of apples from our neighbour's plot.
For ice creams we cajoled, beguiled;
And people, for no reason, smiled
When I was young.

No one thought twice if I forgot
The day of week, or even what
My birth date was – I was a child!
Life was sweet ... it mattered not ...
When I was young.

Curves

Translucent waves, clear, turquoise and curling;
squirrels in tree tops, their soft tails unfurling;

tender young pea shoots, tendrils all tangled;
streams that meander, with waters bright-spangled;

smooth, scalloped edges of butterfly wings;
wriggling flashes of trout fingerlings;

shavings that flow from a wood turner's chisel;
fungi that form with great speed in the drizzle;

honey bee's tongue reaching nectar far down
in a flower; a sleeping mouse, velvety-brown;

coastal paths winding round bays with white sand;
a brightly hued rainbow bent over the land;

a petal, a pebble, a freshwater pearl;
an acorn, a ram's horn, an apple tree burl;
water or storm clouds in eddies or swirls ...
all wonder-full curves in a wonderful world.

Alive

All things seem to thrive in June. This dawn,
the hedgerow's come alive with song, the rising
sun sheds long, strong shadows, spreads warm scents
of must from elderflower; creamy pollen
dusts our hair and noses. Wild roses
interlace with honeysuckle, tracing
patterns through the green. Red campion,
white cow parsley between, rest at their ease;
foxgloves seize their chance ... adopt a stance -
bright-eyed, upright, alert as meerkats,
in habitats of grasslands, forest glades
and moors ... such glorious diversity!
Yes, all things thrive in June, and I,
in tune with them, am come alive.

Poppy

Delicate, crumpled, fragile,
like the wings of a butterfly
newly emerged from its pupa;
humble in its choice of habitat –
roadside verge, cornfield, wasteland;
enlivening with its vivacity –
lifting the hearts of the sad or weary.

No airs or graces,
no desires, or expectations
to be nurtured or tended,
just a wild exuberance,
a zest for life,
a red shout of joy -
to be shared with all
who care to notice.

Nightfall

Light draped itself over the head,
golden-red.
Photographers were out in force,
of course, to stake their pitch,
long eyes trained on the fiery orb
melting slowly into the sea.
Every stone captured an ember,
every grass a slender torch.
The blazing path across the deep
dwindled, and then was gone.
The cameras vanished too.
I alone was left to watch
and wonder, as the hidden sun
backlit the clouds –
a dexterous display
of colour – orange, pink and grey –
till all was monochrome.
I turned for home ...
and found a huge moon hanging high
behind me in a velvet sky.
And with a sigh, I thought, if day
needs must change into night,
this surely is a glorious way.

.

Seeds

Sugar stealers,
silver willow wisps,
thistle down and
dandelion seeds ...
their gentle flight
catches light.
They drift and float
like boats in the air,
carrying cargo
to who knows where ..

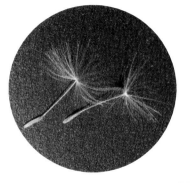

Berry-picking

The slowly westering sun was losing heat
as we turned for home,
laden with harvested treasures.
Berry-stained, sun-sleepy,
burr–encrusted, scratched,
we ate blackberry pancake for tea
as hips and sloes and elderberries
bubbled and glopped on the stove.

Today, in the grip and grey
of winter iciness,
we eat toast, hot and buttered,
with jelly we made that day.
Just for a moment we are back
in that Indian Summer. We hear again
the thrum, the beat, of swans
winging over our heads,
and the hush of the wind-breathed reeds.
We feel the sun-warmed glow envelope us,
and the distant memory of a curlew's call
thrills through us again.

Hallowe'en

Bubbling anticipation fizzes
and tickles their minds.
Pumpkins provide eerie illumination –
a lop-sided zigzag of smile
below piercing eyes.
Ghoulish masks, pointy hats and broomsticks
adorn chattering children
optimistically clutching buckets.
Giggles and shushes ...
a rap on the door ...
will there be sweets? ...
"Trick or treat!"

"Trick or treat ..."
She feels the heat
of anxiety trickle down her brow.
She cowers inside,
lights out, silent,
nothing that might suggest
there is someone at home,
all alone.
Suppressed memories rise to haunt –
memories of dark times ...
memories that mark
and scar her mind.
Evil is near.
She can still hear
and feel it.
Her eyes fill with tears ...
as children's footsteps disappear
into the night.

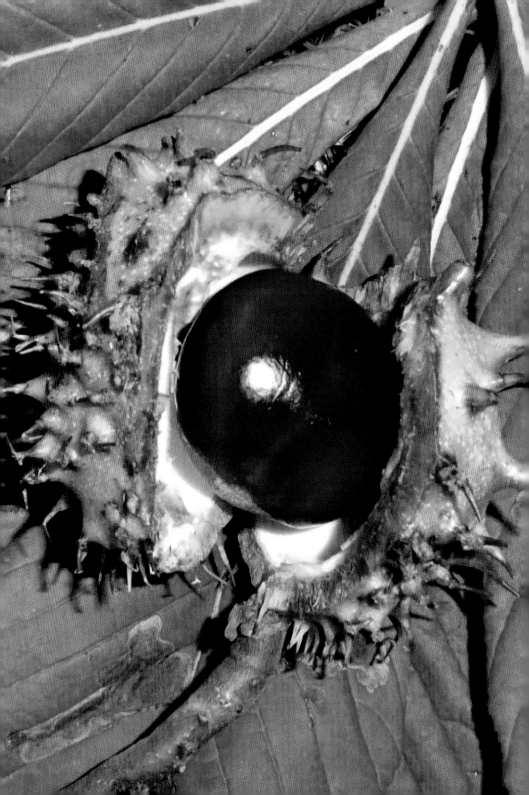

Treasure

A single yellow-crinkled leaf
drifts softly through still air
above my head, as, carefully,
I tread the golden carpet,
deep-piled, rustling at my feet,
the sweet, plump sound
of conkers thudding round me.

Warmth dapples through baring trees
in crisp-cold autumn brightness.
Scents - musty, damp, brown -
fill my nose and mind
as I search, till I find
the richest, roundest,
smoothest, shiniest,
warmest, silkiest,
polished mahogany,
pebble-of-a-conker.

Protected well by spiny armour,
I ease it from its shell
and slip it in my pocket.
All the way home, light of step,
I glow inside, as it hides,
snugly nestled in my hand.

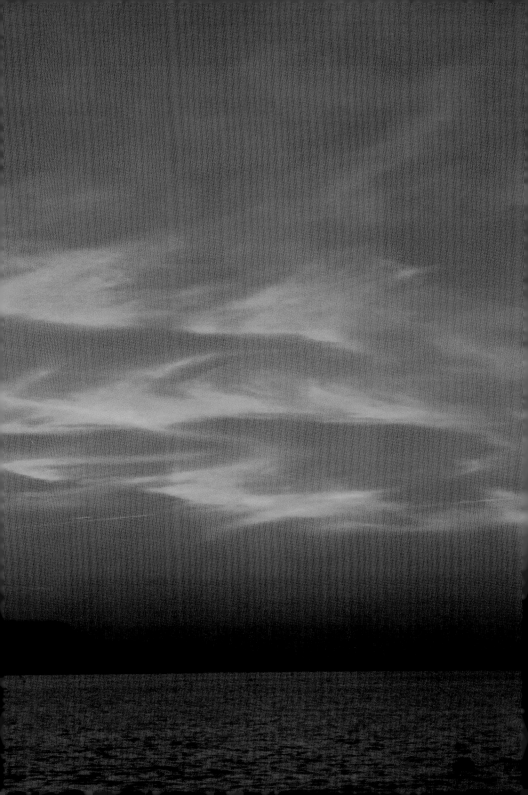

Sunset

A sapphire sky cried winter - brilliant, crisp
and clear, the waning day beckoned, enticed.
Muffling ourselves against the icy cold,
we strolled a golden path past pine trees,
gilded lobster pots and ripples on the shore.
Drawn towards the harbour, mesmerized
by mirror-images of diving gulls,
and dappled water lapping on white hulls,
we stood and watched the slowly sinking sun
touch purple hills and set the sky ablaze,
then disappear. Aurora greens and turquoise
hues suffused the air with blended blues;
and random brushstrokes, orange-hazy-red,
spread glorious streaks of joy above our heads.

Christmas Tree

He took me home, bedecked me
in the finest jewels, put a crown
upon my head, cast presents at my feet.
He caressed my limbs - still evergreen,
still vigorous and vibrant
as the day we first encountered.
He loved me, cared for me,
sang holy songs with me ...
but it was so short-lived.
He whispered, 'Thank you,' then he left,
albeit with a wistful backwards glance.
No chance of a reprieve
on this eve of a new celebration. Maybe
the sudden revelation that he
had no further need of me,
came as my own epiphany.

Interlude

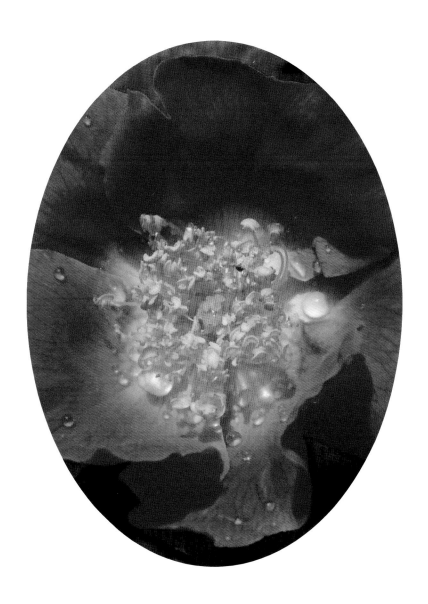

2020

Summer came early that year, but fear
of the virus kept people at home, alone,
each household in strange isolation.
Restaurants, shops, even churches were closed,
though numbers in virtual congregations
rose, as people turned to prayer
and hymns. No meeting of friends for a pint
or a Pimms. No tourists flew in from abroad.
While temperatures soared, the beaches were empty.
Wall to wall sunshine was being recorded,
but we were all ordered to 'stay at home',
to 'stay safe and save the NHS'.
So we missed the best of the weather that year
for fear of the virus which kept us at home.
Some slept to their heart's content, while others
bemoaned the loss of sporting events: no tennis
or football, horse racing or snooker for wasting
a Saturday afternoon. And all
too soon even sailing was vetoed, and camping
was banned as caravan clubs and sites shut their doors.

But ...
out on the moors, wild roses bloomed, scenting
our rooms; nightjars now graced our land, singing
their curious tunes; swallows had flown
to our shores and reported for duty; the country
was covered with all of its seasonal beauty.
Humans were no longer able to roam, but
nature came early, like summer, that year,
with no fear of the virus which kept *us* at home.

Silver Linings
Covid 19 - one perspective

No planes, plying their trade through beleaguered skies;
No trains, (running like clockwork, or otherwise);
No cars, tail-backing on roads, clogging motorways;
No bars, crowded nightclubs or loud, rowdy gigs being played;
No factories belching out plumes of smoke, seeping pollution;
No chemicals, poisons unseen, to affect evolution;
No rushing or pushing or shoving or moving at speed;
No living of life to a deadline, ignoring deep needs.
Instead, time, perhaps, to redress many years of neglect:
Time to value friends, families - demonstrate love and respect;
Time to notice the beauty of nature, its rhythms unchecked;
Time to rethink priorities, care for this world and protect;
Time to savour each moment, to slow down, to pause and reflect;
Time for bodies to rest ... minds, hearts, souls to reconnect.

Make or Break

They say it'll be the making or breaking
of many relationships.
But then, an apple tree cannot grow
unless you break a pip;

no bread could ever be made, unless
the grain was ground down first;
and rainclouds need to appear overhead,
if we would quench our thirst.

Who could create a statue without
chipping away at the stone?
And who knows the value of friendship unless
they have spent some time alone?

There's pain and strain aplenty before
a beautiful baby is born;
and everyone knows the saying that goes,
'The dark hour is just before dawn.'

Though these are tough old times of great
uncertainty, who knows ...
it could be just that brokenness
from which a future grows.

When, if not now?

Is now the time?
Is this the opportunity
the world's been waiting for?
Could we, should we, use this global crisis,
this international calamity
to jump in with both feet,
to leap into the breach,
to bite the bullet (better yet,
to ban it)? Will there ever be
another chance? Could every nation
join the dance of all creation –
one together to weather storms,
to cancel debts; forgive, forget; to, maybe,
take a bigger step - uniting
globally to fight a common
enemy, and not each other;
to recognise each person as
a mother, sister, brother?
Is now the time to choose love over greed;
the time to 'do no harm'; the time
for unilateral disarmament;
the time to meet the needs of earth
and all upon it? More than just
the stuff of sonnets, can love be
the stuff of true reality, where life
is simply lived, to benefit
the common good. Could this be how
we thrive, come wholly alive?
I think it could ... and if not now, then when?

Seas

All I Need

A moment or two along the sea wall,
a sunset and a curlew's call
is all that I need to nourish my soul,
to bring me peace, to make me whole.

Coastal Path

Bright with promise, that September day,
my feet led the way, as they often do,
to the shell beach. The ebbing tide
had left behind small cockle cups
of trapped sunshine. The marsh nearby
was samphire-red. A lazy day.
Michaelmas daisies purpled the path;
yellow-wellied egrets stepped,
keeping elegant time with their necks;
dunlin speckled the shallows,
playing tag along the muddy shore,
then rose as one – like a silver shoal of fish,
twisting, deflecting, reflecting light and dark.
Stray, wispy clouds highlighted
distant ups and downs, away beyond
the silver Solent ribbon. White sails drifted,
lifted and fell with the swell.
Canada geese and Brenties honked and burbled;
seagulls argued the toss as to who was boss;
cows lowed in the distance; curlews called
insistently; the tiny click of turnstones
flecked the soundscape. Nature noises drowned
those made by humankind.
Time to unwind ...

Exhilaration

Storms lashed the coast...
But, while others curled up
in front of the fire,
eating hot-buttered toast,
my brother and I donned wellies
and coats – needing to be outside.
Heads bowed against an unseen force,
following a course along the head,
flying the wind, arms outspread
as we walked. We could not talk –
could only shout.

Icy rain and hail
flailed us from blackened skies;
wind whipped up white peaks on puddles;
cattle, sad and muddled
by the mad weather, huddled together.
I watched my brother,
(so usually-calm-and-mild)
watched him come alive –
a wild, bright joy in his eyes –
exhilaration fed by wild seas, wild skies.

By the Way

And as you walk the coastal path,
between salt marsh and silver Solent,
don't hurry ... take your time ...
allow the rhyme and rhythm of the sea
free rein in you. Close your eyes.
Internalise reflections of red-gold streaked skies.
Listen for the widgeon's squeal.
Feel cool winds tingle your face.
Trace finger patterns in the sand.
Let your lungs expand.
Hear the thrum of winging swans,
high-singing larks, the geese contented burbling,
while a curlew's rippling call
slips through the wall around your heart.

When the Tide went Out

What a joy it was to meet
The boy (aged 4?) whose little feet
Felt 'cosy' in the slippy weed -
Bright and green, left by the sea
When the tide went out.

'Where would you hide, if you were a crab?'
Engaging questions from his dad
Brought heads together, bent down low,
Looking for where a crab might go
When the tide went out.

Coming to my Senses

I look and look, then close my eyes,
trying to lock this image in my mind
against a time I might be blind.

Sunshine warms my face; sands shift
beneath cold toes where water laps;
hair tousled by a gentle breeze.

And, eyes still closed, I breathe in deep.
Salt air, seaweed, and a hint
of sweet wild roses reach my nose.

Sea susurrates along the shore;
a skylark pours her song on me;
and longing captures memory.

Haiku

Haunting curlew call
Echoes the deepest yearning
Of my hungry soul

Water

Without water there would be
no whisky, wine, no beer or tea.
Nothing would grow – no beans or peas,
no apples, plums or strawberries;
no blossom-laden plants or trees.
There'd be no frogs or chimpanzees;
no skylarks, no long skeins of geese.
No fish-shaped clouds, no mist to please
artistic eyes – no poetry.
No waterfalls, no estuaries;
there'd be no river-walks to ease
the troubled mind and bring it peace.
There'd be no surfing, wild and free;
no puddle-jumping splashily;
no sailing on sun-sparkling seas
stretching to infinity.
Nothing would love or laugh or be ...
no life on earth, no you or me.

Peace

A luminous day, light-filled, air-stilled,
draws me to the marshes.
Grasses, teasels, reeds, all
twinned in motionless water.
Herons poise, elegantly mirrored;
skeins of geese skim past cloud-wisps –
a double image, above and below.
Light-catching gossamer threads
float lazily. Eyes close,
sun warms, mind drifts hazily.
Fresh seaweed fragrances salt air.
I dare to unwind. Silence-seeking,
I sit on the shore
wanting nothing more
than peace.

Keyhaven

I push out the bows, let the wind fill her sail
I'm free as a bird – every stress is exhaled ...

Waves lapping gently against the hull
Flocks of hungry herring gulls,
Swans beat their wings, flying higher and higher.
Burbling geese rest amidst the samphire,
Sunshine reflecting like millions of stars,
Overfalls marking the shallow sand bars,
Whitewashed lighthouse against clear azure sky
(Permanent grin on my face – can't think why!)
A quick flash of blue where a kingfisher darts
And the call of the curlew quickens my heart;
The wind's in my face and I'm covered with spray
All's right with the world on this beautiful day!
Awash with happiness ... I am afloat
In the very best place to be sailing a boat!

Weather

Working itself up into a fury,
the weather wailed, throwing stones,
flotsam, boats and beach huts
all skywards and into fields beyond.

Next morning, fury spent,
sun shone from a blue sky on a still day ...
like a tantrum-throwing toddler
tossing toys from a cot, who, having got
everyone's attention, becomes all sweetness
and light, and butter-wouldn't-melt-in-the-mouth.

Lymington Marshes

On a quest for quiet, I head west
on the coastal path, pursuing peace -
unfettered by conversation.

The geese know better! Their burble
brings an unexpected smile, while
wading birds chatter, and scatter
stones as they feast along the water's edge.
The sea breathes softly, rhythmically
hushing the shingle;
a tingle of anticipation appears.

Ears, now attuned to nature's symphony, hear
swans' wings beat in resonant synchrony.
Wigeons' shrill warnings, a gull's plaintive mews
accompany cows with their barber-shop moos.

And overriding all, the pure clear call
of a sky-high lark. A crescendo
of exultation reaches for my heart ...
turns it inside out.

Seagull

I close my eyes ... and I am soaring
high above the shoreline;
following cliff edges,
skimming ledges;
riding the wind, gliding
effortlessly against
gentian blue -
sky above, sea below.
No limitation, pure elation,
exhilaration, liberation ...
and intimations of immanence.
Soft and soundless,
saying not a word,
I am free. Free as a bird.

Ebb tide

I watched the tide go out today.
A stiff wind blew in gusts,
sun-silvered reeds flashed a Mexican wave,
a murmuration of wind flitted, skittered
across the face of the water.

I watched the tide go out.
Mud flats emerged before my very eyes,
puddles reflected the skies
like jigsaw pieces waiting to be fitted.
Sunshine warmed my back
and cast a shadow, dark across
stark heads of cow parsley, wild grasses,
bladder wrack in tousled tresses.

I watched the tide go out,
while distant clouds above the island
birthed a double rainbow from their depths.
I listened to a swan's pulsating wings
fade softly westwards;
heard squabbling gulls,
like children on a playground;
was spell-bound by the sound
of curlew calls.

I watched the tide go out today,
and I was blessed by inactivity.

Open Space

If ever you're faced with adversity,
a wild open space will set your soul free;
a place to replenish, where you can 'just be' ...
whether mountain or moorland, forest or sea.

Thanks

To anyone who has ever made any murmurs of affirmation about my poems, I would like to express my heartfelt gratitude. To David, Vanessa, Jan and Maggie – thank you so much for your thoughts and gentle suggestions. And to Margaret and Marguerite – thank you for leading the group which started me on this path.